Name _____

Who Is My Motl

Trace the path from each baby to its mom.
Color the pictures.

Try This! Make the sound each animal makes.

1

Back to the Nest

Trace the path from each bird back to the nest.
Color the picture.

Try This! Name three kinds of birds.

2

Road Race

Follow the maze to the Finish Line.

Try This! Draw something that is faster than a car.

FS-32055 Kindergarten Review

Tunnel

Help the prairie dog find its way home.
Draw the path.

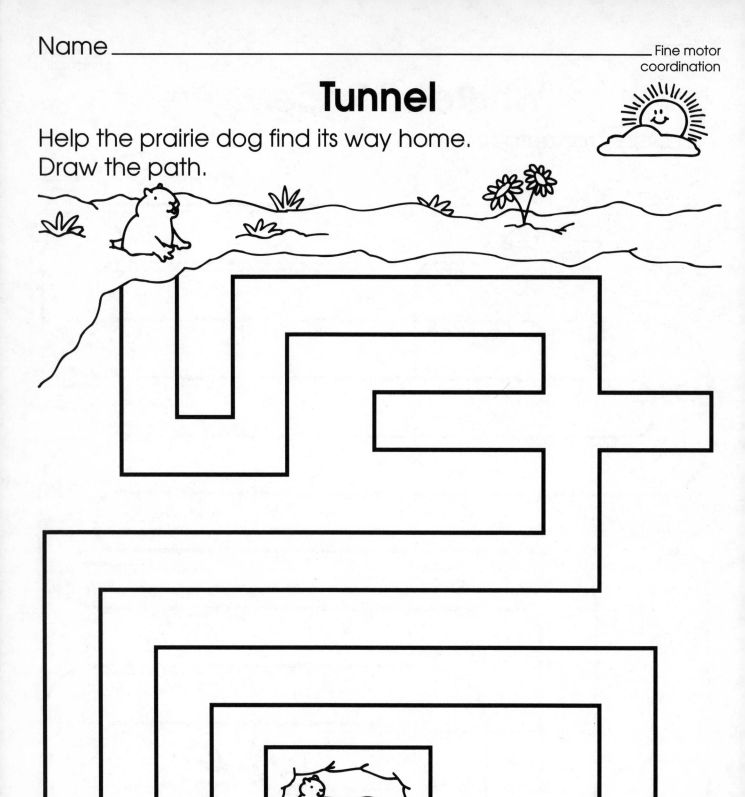

Try This! Draw another animal that lives underground.

FS-32055 Kindergarten Review

Where's My Cave?

Help the dragon find its cave.
Draw the path.

Cave

Try This! Do you think dragons are real? Tell why.

FS-32055 Kindergarten Review

Under the Sea

Help the starfish find its starfish family.
Draw the path.

Try This! How many starfish are on this page? _____

    FS-32055 Kindergarten Review

All Kinds of Leaves

Trace each leaf.
Color.

Try This! Draw a tree with leaves.

7

Animal Shapes

Trace each animal.

Try This! Color the animals you have seen.

8

Draw What's Missing

Draw the missing parts.

Try This! Draw one of these pictures on the back of the page.

FS-32055 Kindergarten Review

Finish the Pictures

Finish each picture to match.

Try This! Draw most of an animal. Let a friend finish it.

Alike and Different

Color the pictures that are alike.
Draw an **X** on the picture that is different.

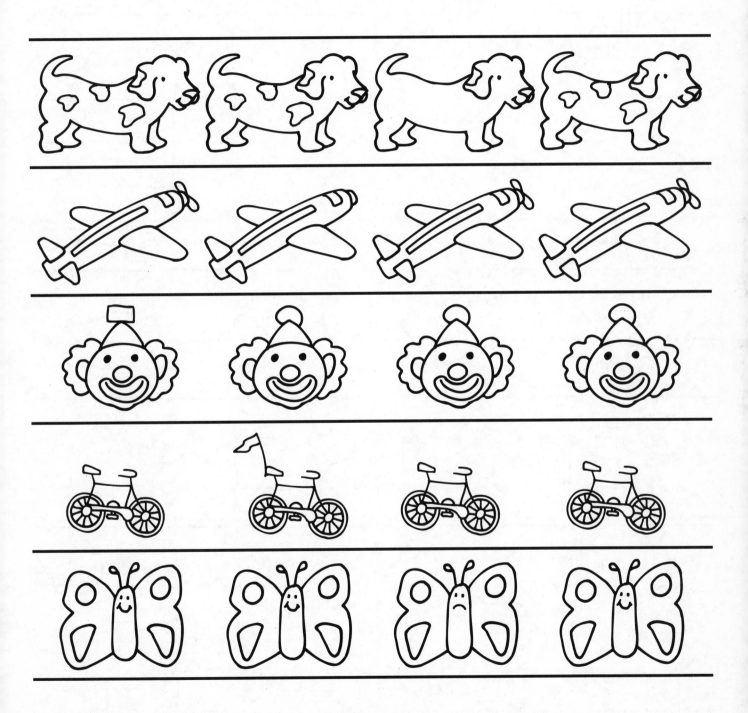

Try This! Choose a row. Draw a picture to match.

11

Name_____

At the Farm

Color the animals that are alike.
Draw an **X** on the animal that is different.

Try This! Draw another animal that lives on a farm.

12

FS-32055 Kindergarten Review

Pumpkin Patch

Draw lines between the matching pumpkins.

Try This! Draw a happy pumpkin.

FS-32055 Kindergarten Review

All Kinds of Vegetables

Draw lines between the matching vegetables.

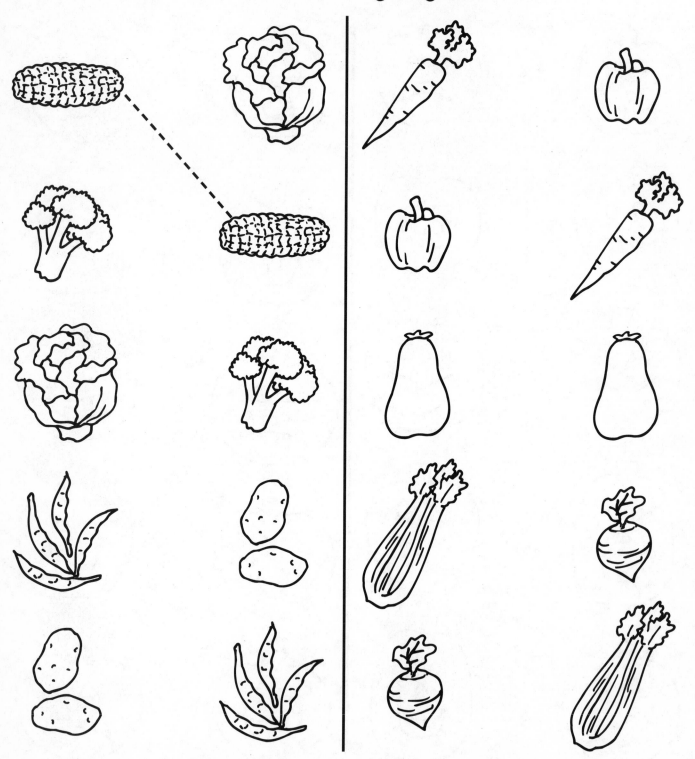

Try This! Color the vegetables you like to eat.

14

Name_____

*Visual
discrimination*

Shadow Fun

Match each picture to its shadow.

Try This! Look at your shadow every recess. How does it change?

Truck Shadows

Match each truck to its shadow.

Try This! Which of these trucks can you name?

FS-32055 Kindergarten Review

Writing Uppercase Letters
Color, trace, and write each letter.

A A ____ ____   H H ____ ____

B B ____ ____   I I ____ ____

C C ____ ____   J J ____ ____

D D ____ ____   K K ____ ____

E E ____ ____   L L ____ ____

F F ____ ____   M M ____ ____

G G ____ ____   N N ____ ____

Try This! Use your finger to write each letter in the air.

FS-32055 Kindergarten Review

Name _____

More Uppercase Letters
Color, trace, and write each letter.

O O _____ U U _____

P P _____ V V _____

Q Q _____ W W _____

R R _____ X X _____

S S _____ Y Y _____

T T _____ Z Z _____

Try This! Use your finger to write each letter in the air.

18

Writing Lowercase Letters
Color, trace, and write each letter.

a a _____ _____

b b _____ _____

c c _____ _____

d d _____ _____

e e _____ _____

f f _____ _____

g g _____ _____

h h _____ _____

i i _____ _____

j j _____ _____

k k _____ _____

l l _____ _____

m m _____ _____

n n _____ _____

Try This! For each pair of letters, circle the one you wrote neater.

19

More Lowercase Letters
Color, trace, and write each letter.

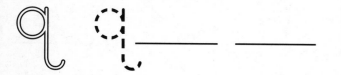

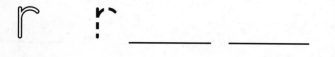

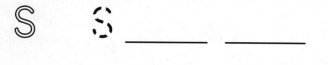

Try This! For each pair of letters, circle the one you wrote neater.

In the Woods

Connect the dots from **A** to **Z**.

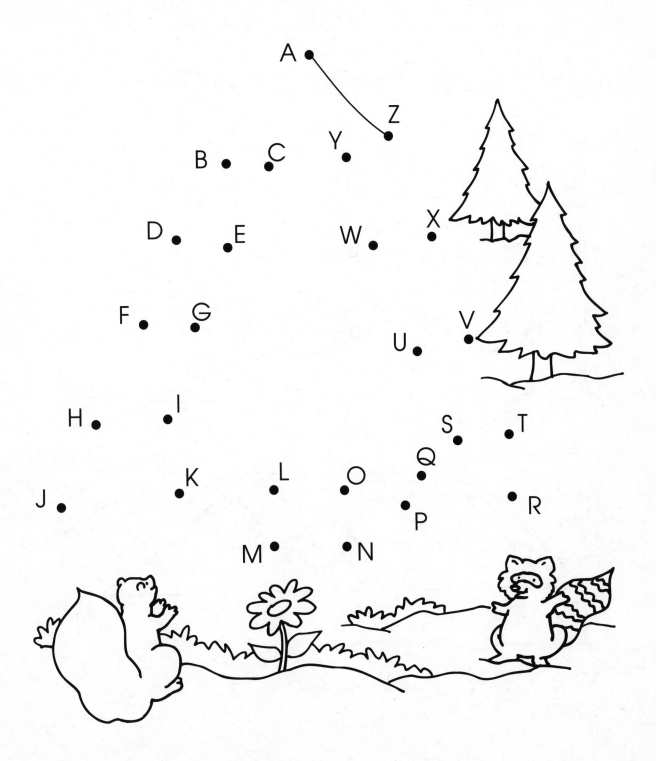

Try This! Point to each letter as you quietly sing the alphabet.

FS-32055 Kindergarten Review

At the Park

Connect the dots from **A** to **Z**.

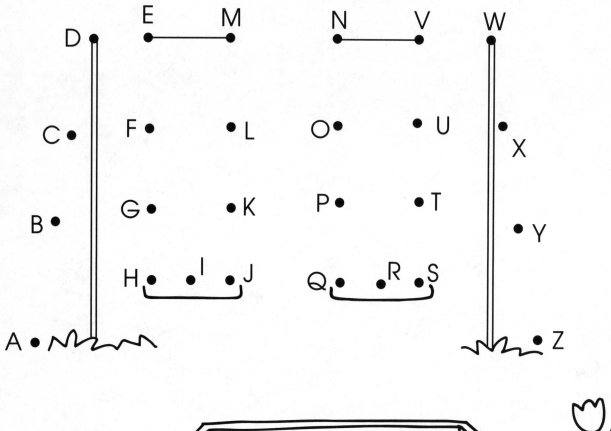

Try This! Choose a letter. How many names can you think of that start with that letter?

22

What Is It?

Connect the dots from **a** to **z**.

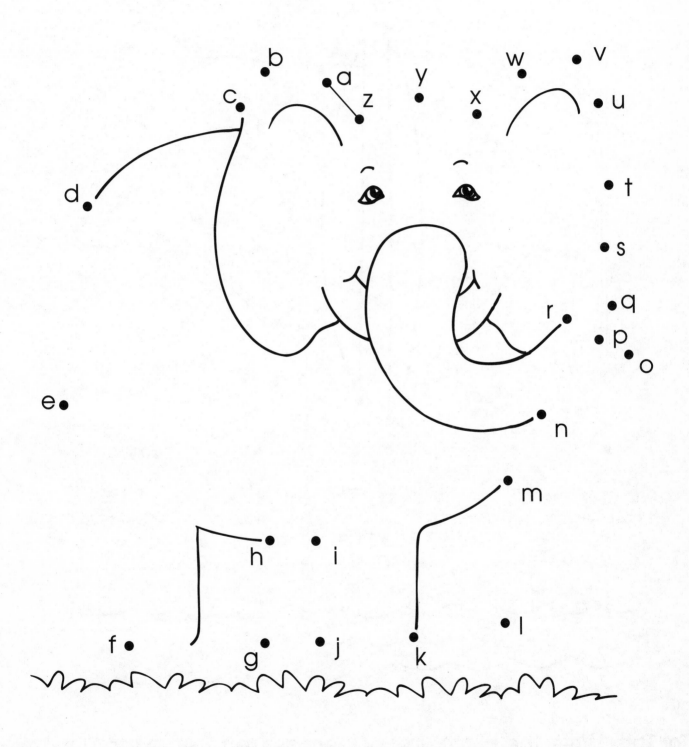

Try This! Point to each letter as you say the alphabet.

FS-32055 Kindergarten Review

Sailing, Sailing

Connect the dots from **a** to **z**.

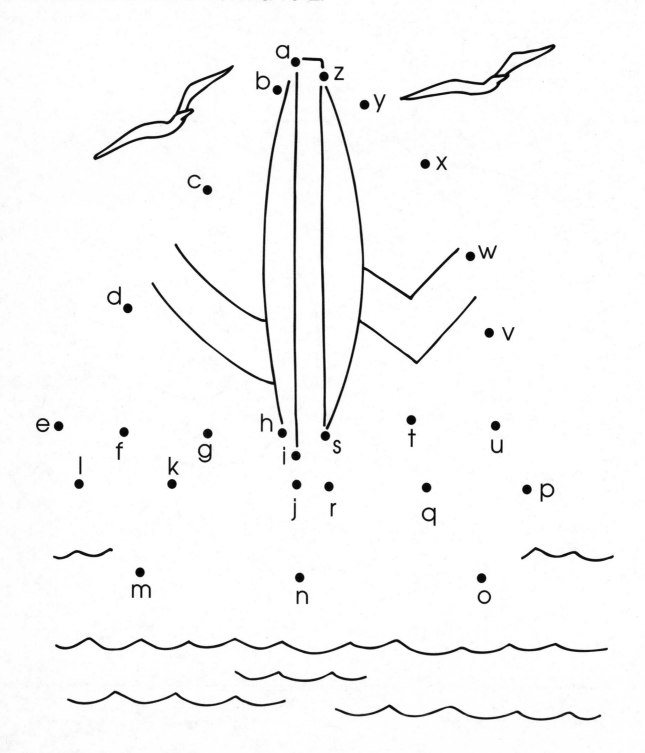

Try This! Write the matching uppercase letters next to
the lowercase letters.

24

Alphabet Match-up
Draw lines to match the letters.

a	C	n	K	s	U
b	A	k	L	t	V
c	D	l	J	u	S
d	B	m	N	v	W
e	F	j	P	w	T
f	E	o	M	x	Z
g	I	p	O	y	X
h	H	q	R	z	Y
i	G	r	Q		

Try This! Which letter pairs look alike? Which look different?

25

FS-32055 Kindergarten Review

A Bunch of Balloons
Draw lines to match the letters.

Try This! Color the balloon that has the first letter of your name.

FS-32055 Kindergarten Review

Alphabet Practice

Read the letters. Write the letters.

Aa   Bb

Cc   Dd

Ee   Ff

Gg   Hh

Ii   Jj

Kk   Ll

Mm   Nn

Try This! Trace over each set of letters with a crayon.

          FS-32055 Kindergarten Review

More Alphabet Practice

Read the letters. Write the letters.

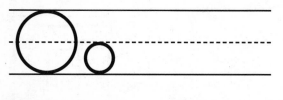
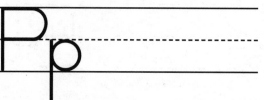
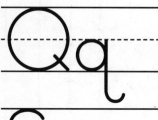
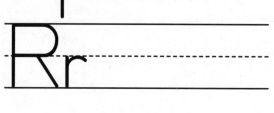

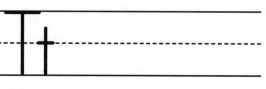
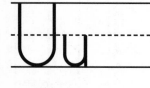

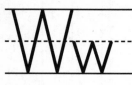
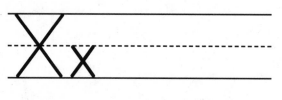

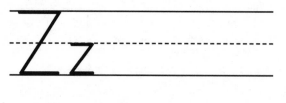
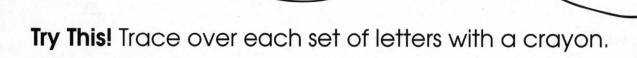

Try This! Trace over each set of letters with a crayon.

FS-32055 Kindergarten Review

Alphabet Squares

Write the missing uppercase letters in the big box.
Then trace over all the letters with a crayon.

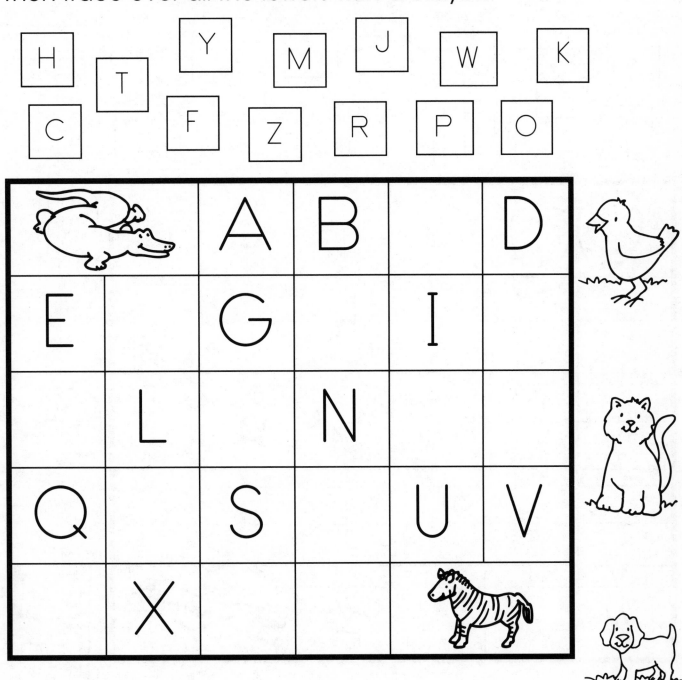

Try This! Play this game: Close your eyes. Point to a letter.
Open your eyes. Say the letter.

Alphabet Fun

Write the missing lowercase letters in the big box.
Then trace over all the letters with a crayon.

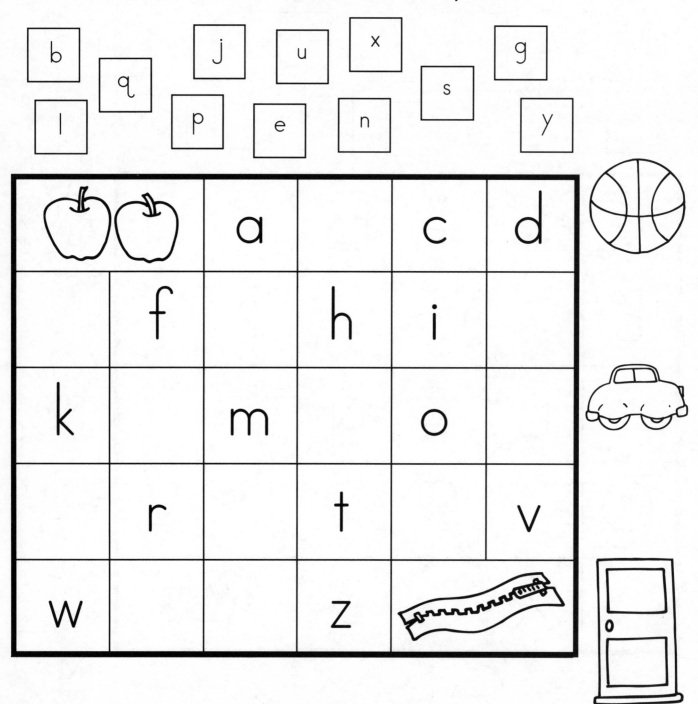

b   j   u   x   g
q
l   p   e   n   s   y

	a		c	d
	f		h	i
k		m		o
	r		t	v
w			z	

Try This! Look at the letters. Which ones are made with only straight lines? Which ones are made with only curved lines?

FS-32055 Kindergarten Review

Alphabet Critter

Write the letters from **A** to **Z**.

Try This! Draw an alphabet critter that spells out your name.

31

What a Worm!

Write the letters from **a** to **z**.

a b

g

o

w

Try This! Point to the letters as you say the alphabet backwards.

Missing Letters

Write the missing letters.

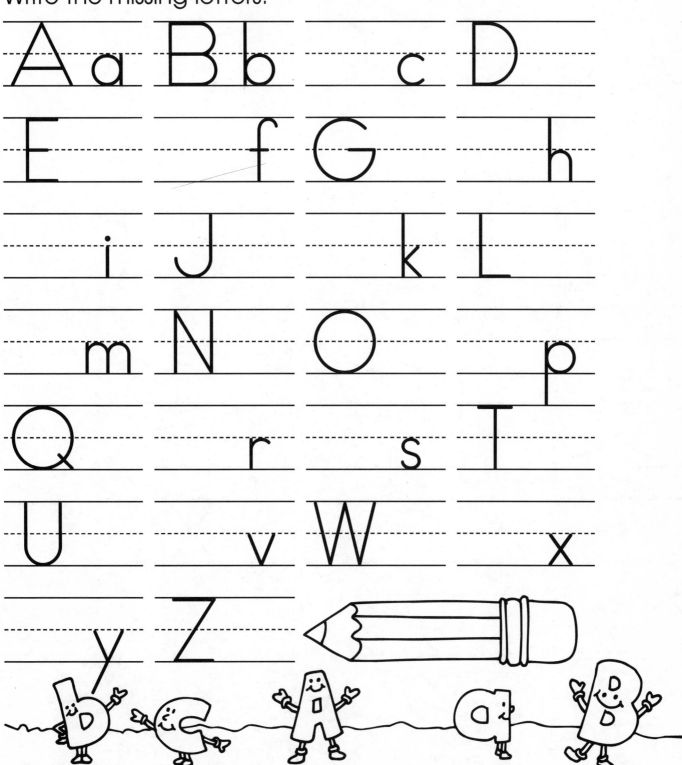

A a   B b   c   D

E   f   G   h

i   J   k   L

m   N   O   p

Q   r   s   T

U   v   W   x

y   Z

Try This! Play this game with a friend. Use a finger to write a letter in the air. Have your friend name it.

FS-32055 Kindergarten Review

Aa to Zz

Write the missing letters.

Aa   C

       F

               I

               Oo

               X

       Z

Try This! Use a finger to write a lowercase letter on a friend's hand. Have your friend write the matching uppercase letter.

FS-32055 Kindergarten Review

Matching Sounds

Draw lines between the pictures that begin with the same sound.

Try This! Draw two things that begin with the same sound.

35

Animal Match-up

Draw lines between the animals that begin with the same sound.

Try This! Name an animal that starts with the letter **b**.

FS-32055 Kindergarten Review

Name _____

Ball, Book, and Butterfly

Circle the pictures that start with the sound shown.
Draw an **X** on the picture that doesn't match.

Try This! Choose a row. Draw a new picture to match.

FS-32055 Kindergarten Review

Turtle, Top, and Ten

Circle the pictures that start with the sound shown.
Draw an **X** on the picture that doesn't match.

t			
n			
l			
q			
f			
g			
j			

Try This! Choose a row. Draw a new picture to match.

What Sound Does It Start With?

Look at the picture. What sound does it start with?
Circle the matching letter. Color the picture.

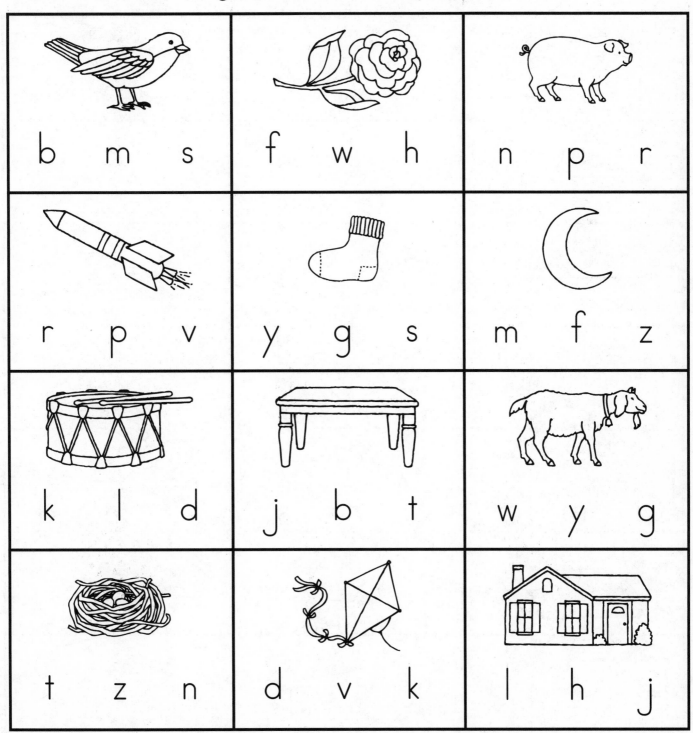

b m s	f w h	n p r
r p v	y g s	m f z
k l d	j b t	w y g
t z n	d v k	l h j

Try This! Draw three pictures that begin with the same sound.

What's the Sound?

Look at the picture. What sound does it start with?
Circle the matching letter. Color the picture.

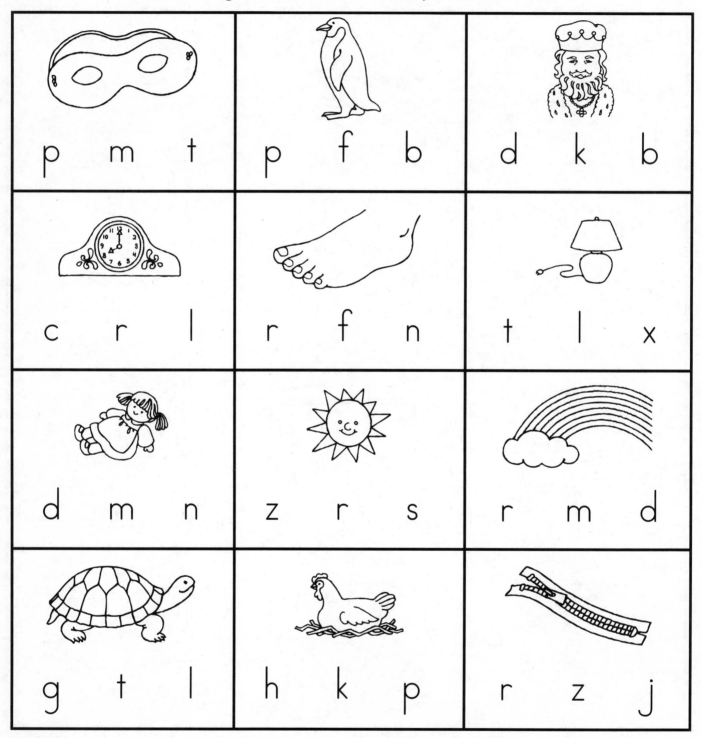

p m t	p f b	d k b
c r l	r f n	t l x
d m n	z r s	r m d
g t l	h k p	r z j

Try This! Draw a picture of something that begins with **z**.

40

What's the Letter?

Look at the pictures. Write the beginning sound.

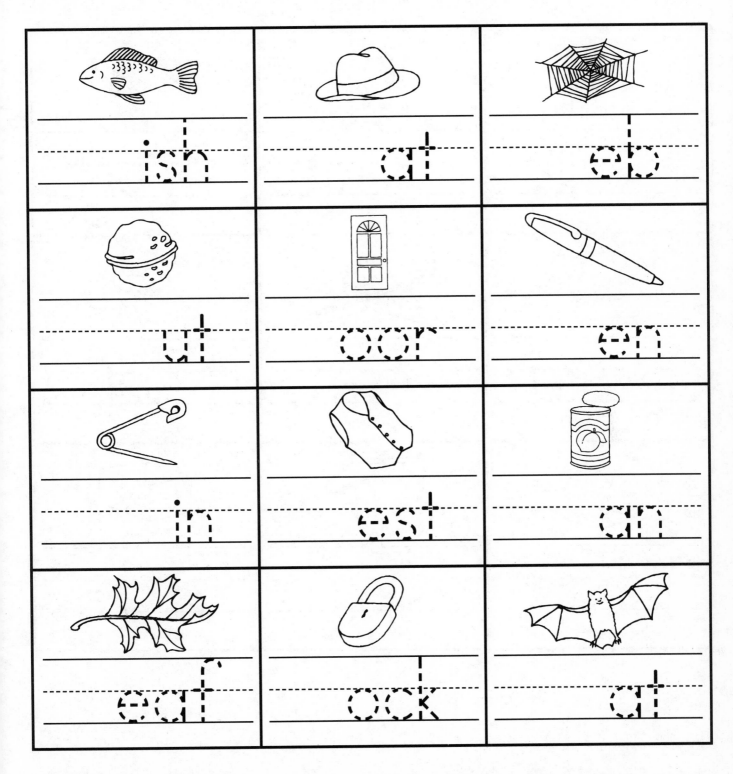

Try This! Draw a picture of an animal that begins with **f**.

FS-32055 Kindergarten Review

What Comes First?

Look at the pictures. Write the beginning sound.

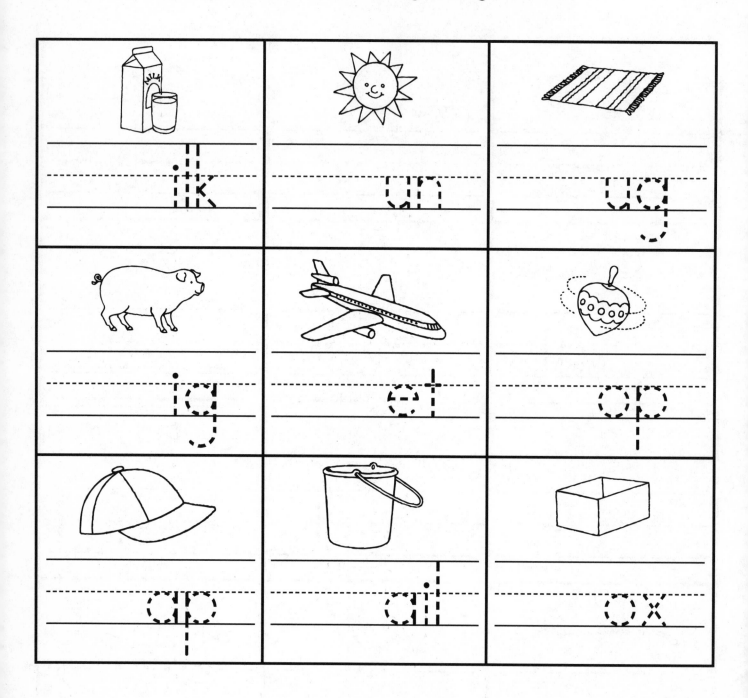

ilk

un

ug

ig

et

op

ap

ail

ox

Try This! Think of five things that begin with **w**.

Make a Match

Draw lines to match the pictures to the sounds.

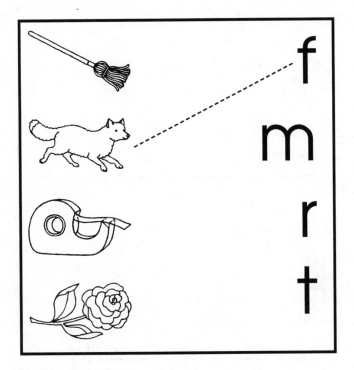

Try This! Name two toys that begin with **b.**

Making Pictures

Draw pictures that begin with the sounds.

b	v
z	p
r	l
t	f

Try This! Pick a letter. Make a picture for that letter. Have a friend guess which letter you chose.

44

Name _____

Colors

Trace. Write. Color.

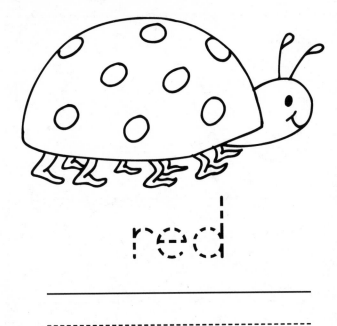

red

_____

blue

_____

black

_____

orange

_____

Try This! Find these colors in your room.

More Colors

Trace. Write. Color.

green

_____

- - - - - - - - - - - -

_____

brown

_____

- - - - - - - - - - - -

_____

purple

_____

- - - - - - - - - - - -

_____

yellow

_____

- - - - - - - - - - - -

_____

Try This! Find these colors in your room.

Colorful Crayons

Trace and color.

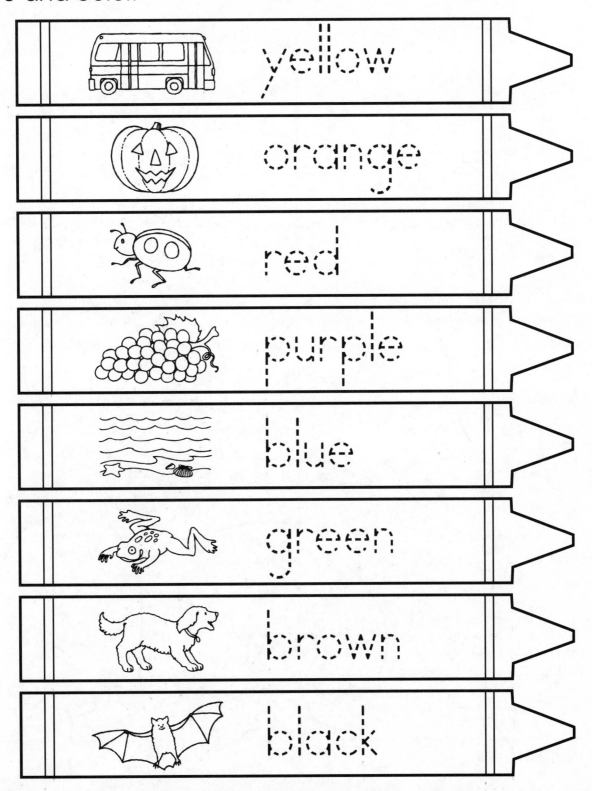

Try This! Draw a ★ by the colors you are wearing today.

47

FS-32055 Kindergarten Review

Monster Colors

Trace and color.

Try This! Draw a monster with your favorite color crayon.

Name _____

Rainy Day

Color.

blue   orange   blue   orange

brown

black

brown

brown

yellow

green

red

purple

Try This! What colors would you like on an umbrella?

49

Little Red Riding Hood

Color.

Try This! Draw a different outfit for Little Red Riding Hood to wear that isn't red. Then give her a new name.

50

The Rain Forest

Color.

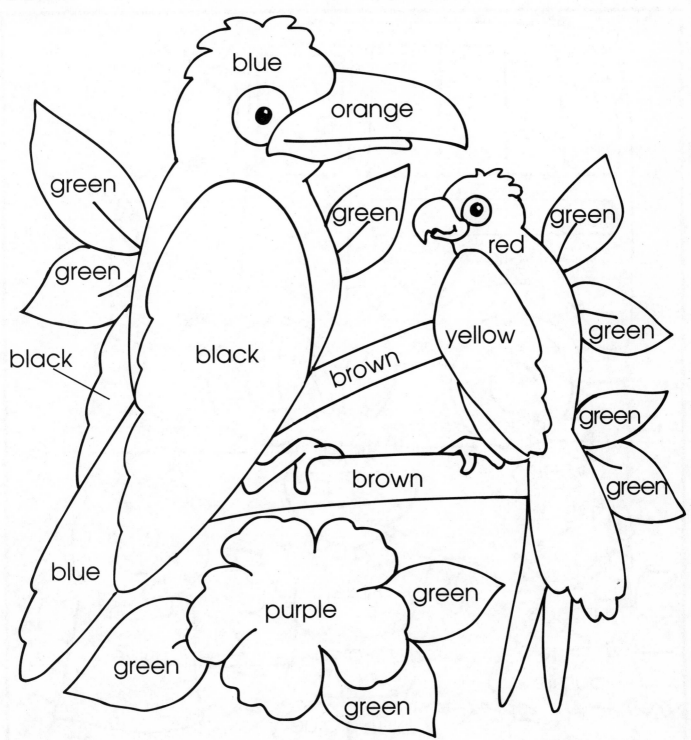

Try This! Name an animal that lives in the rain forest. What color is it?

51

Name _____

Time for School

Color.

yellow

black

black

orange

purple

green

brown

blue

blue

blue

green

red

red

Try This! Color a picture of you going to school.

FS-32055 Kindergarten Review

What Color Is It?

Match. Color.

 - - - - - - - - - purple

red

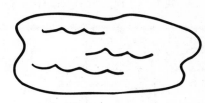

blue

green

black

yellow

brown

orange

Try This! Name a color that isn't on this page.

53

Many Colors

Draw an **X** on the color that doesn't belong.
Color the pictures.

---

leaves   green   brown   purple

---

apples   red   yellow   black

---

cats   orange   green   black

---

grapes   orange   purple   green

---

water   red   green   blue

Try This! Draw fish of many colors.

FS-32055 Kindergarten Review

Name _____

Circles

Trace.   Draw.

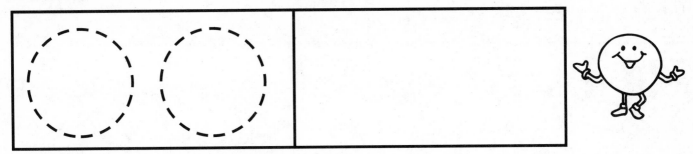

Color only the circles.

Try This! Draw a picture with circles in it.

55

Find the Circles

Trace.

circle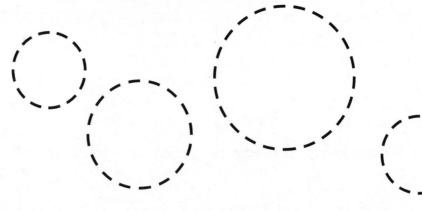

Color only the circles.

Try This! Draw three circles.

Squares

Trace. Draw.

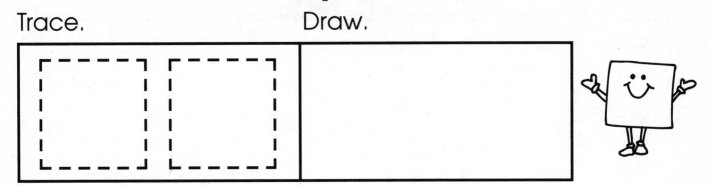

Color only the squares.

Try This! Draw a picture with squares in it.

Find the Squares

Trace.

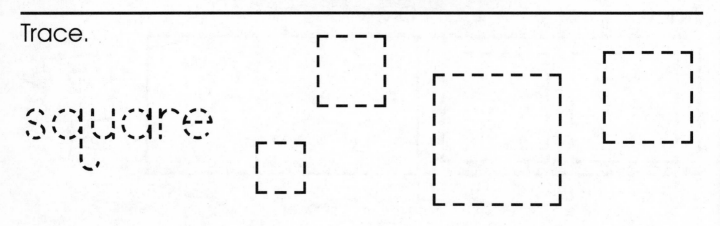

square

Color only the squares.

Try This! Draw three squares.

58

Triangles

Trace. Draw.

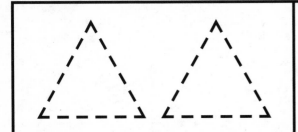 

Color only the triangles.

Try This! Draw a picture with triangles in it.

FS-32055 Kindergarten Review

Find the Triangles

Trace.

triangle

Color only the triangles.

Try This! Draw three triangles.

FS-32055 Kindergarten Review

Name _____

Rectangles

Trace.   Draw.

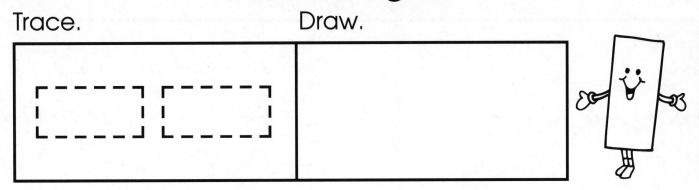

Color only the rectangles.

Try This! Draw a picture with rectangles in it.

61

Name _____

Find the Rectangles

Trace.

rectangle

Color only the rectangles.

Try This! Draw three rectangles.

Lots of Shapes

Trace.   Draw.

oval

diamond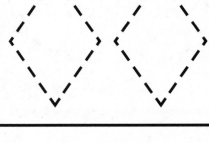

heart

star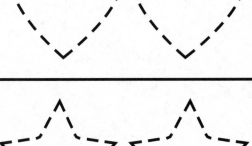

Try This! Draw a funny face using these four shapes.

63

FS-32055 Kindergarten Review

Shapes

Trace. Color.

oval

diamond

star

heart

Try This! Draw two of each shape.

Juggling Fun

Color:

◯ red   ☐ blue   △ green   ▭ yellow

Try This! Draw yourself juggling four orange balls.

    FS-32055 Kindergarten Review

Home Sweet Home

Color:

◯ yellow ▭ green △ red ☐ blue

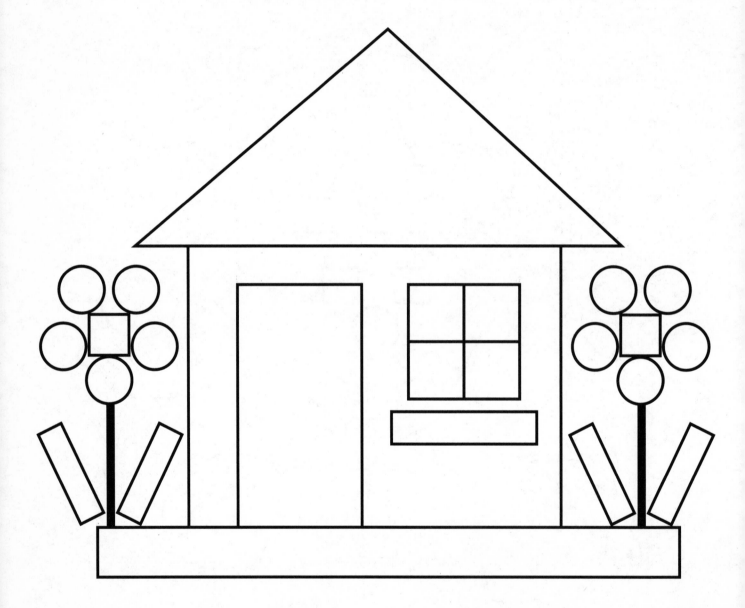

Try This! Draw and color a picture of your home.

Spring Flowers

Color:

◯ yellow △ green ☐ black ◇ blue

☆ purple ⬭ orange ▭ brown ♡ red

Try This! Choose three colors and three shapes.
Draw a flower using only those colors and shapes.

A Tile Design

Color:

◯ yellow   ▭ green   ◇ black   △ blue

♡ purple   ⬭ orange   ▢ brown   ☆ red

Try This! Draw your own tile design. Make the same shapes the same color.

68

Color Patterns

Color. Finish the pattern. **R**=Red **B**=Blue **G**=Green

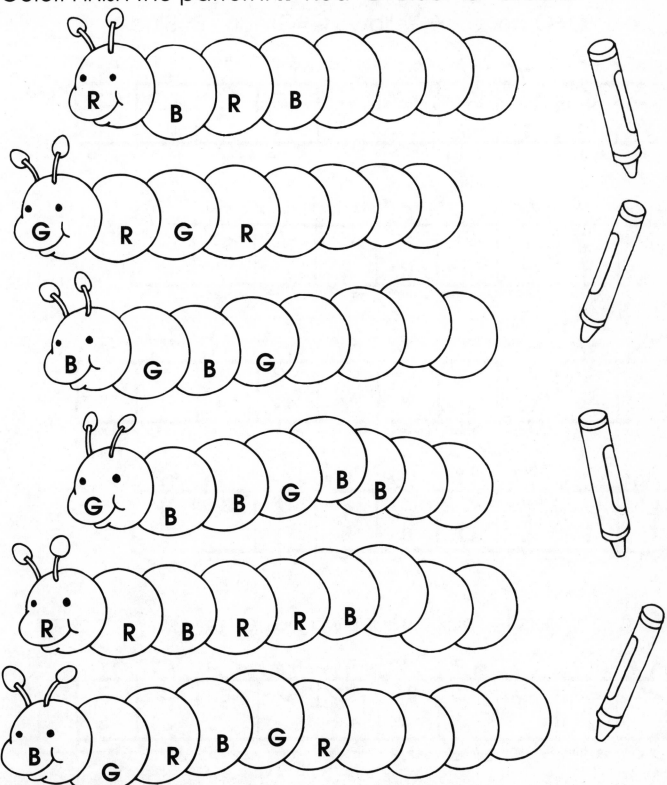

Try This! Draw your own color pattern worm.

FS-32055 Kindergarten Review

Pattern People

Color. Finish the pattern.

R=Red **O**=Orange **Y**=Yellow **G**=Green **B**=Blue

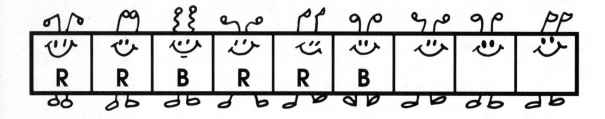

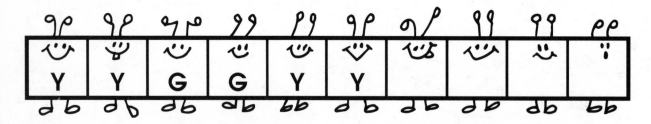

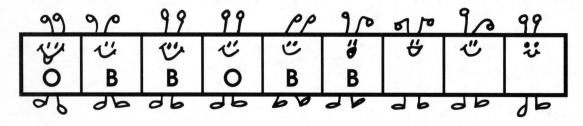

Use two colors to make your own pattern.

Try This! Make a color pattern using three colors.

FS-32055 Kindergarten Review

Shape Patterns

Say the pattern aloud. Draw the missing shapes.

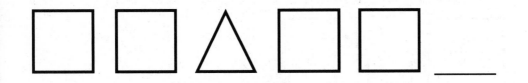

Choose two shapes. Draw your own pattern.

Try This! Draw a pattern with three shapes:

71

FS-32055 Kindergarten Review

What Shape Comes Next?

Say the pattern aloud. Draw the missing shapes.

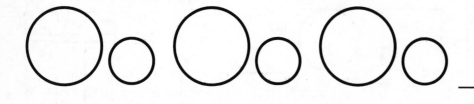

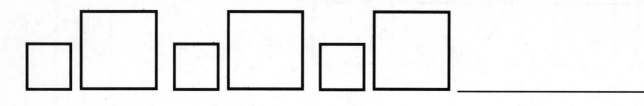

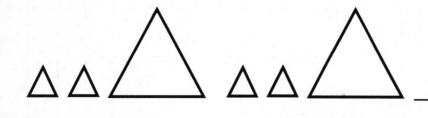

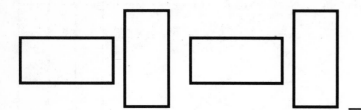

Draw your own shape pattern.

Try This! Draw a pattern with happy faces and sad faces.

Name _____

Writing Numbers 1 to 5
Count. Trace. Write.

• ┆ ┆

••

•••

•••• ᴴ ᴴ

••••• 5 5

Try This! Circle the number you wrote best in each row.

FS-32055 Kindergarten Review

Writing Numbers 6 to 10
Count. Trace. Write.

6   6

7   7

8   8

9   9

10   10

Try This! Circle the number you wrote best in each row.

FS-32055 Kindergarten Review

Name_____

Writing 1 to 10

Color, trace, and write each number.

1 1	6 6
2 2	7 7
3 3	8 8
4 4	9 9
5 5	10 10

1 2 3 4 5 6 7 8 9 10

Try This! Write how old you are.

75

FS-32055 Kindergarten Review

Twins

Trace. Write the number on the matching animal.

Try This! Draw an animal. Write your favorite number on it.

FS-32055 Kindergarten Review

Desert Life

Color **2**.

Color **4**.

Color **1**.

Color **3**.

Color **5**.

Color **6**.

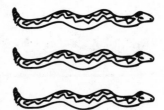

Color **8**.

Color **7**.

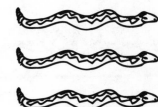

Try This! How many legs does a tarantula have?

FS-32055 Kindergarten Review

Ocean Animals

Color **3**.

Color **7**.

Color **4**.

Color **8**.

Color **6**.

Color **9**.

Try This! Draw 10 fish. Color 2 of them.

78

Out in Space

Count. Write the number.

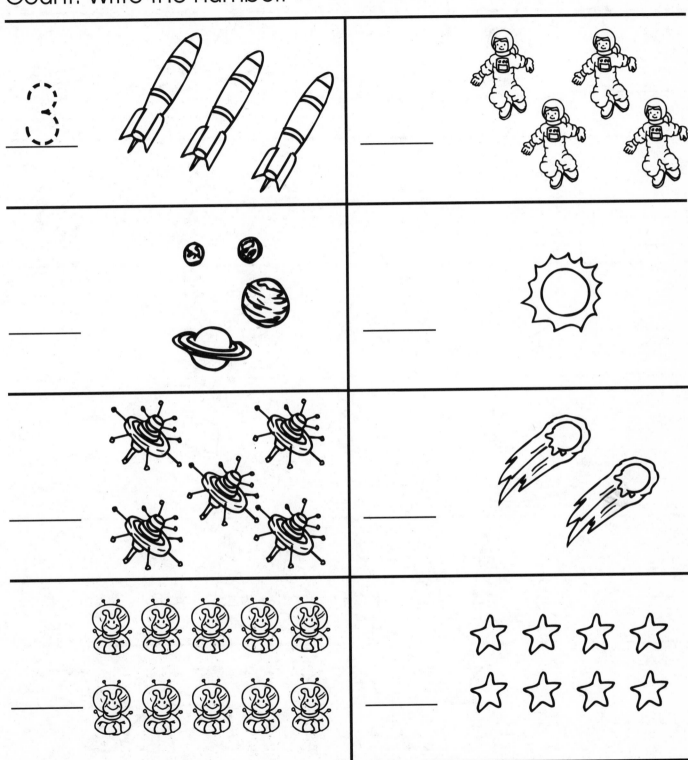

Try This! Draw 5 friends in a rocket.

FS-32055 Kindergarten Review

Name_____

Hats Off!

Count. Write the number.

4

___

___

___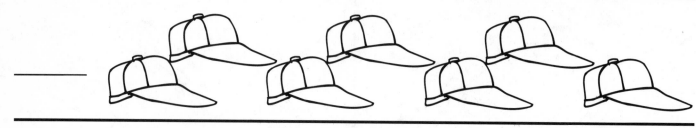

___

___

Try This! Draw yourself wearing a stack of 6 caps.

80

A Writing Tool

Connect the dots from **1** to **10**.

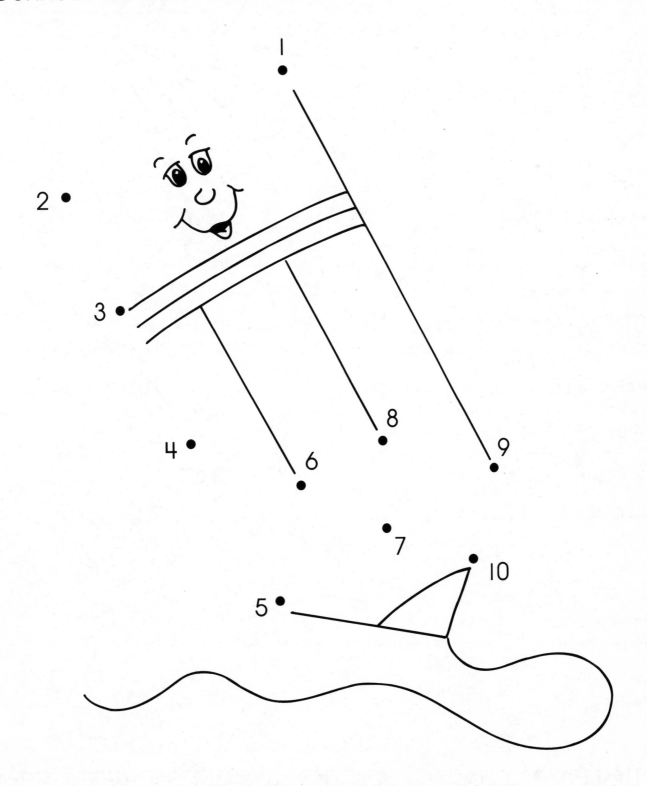

Try This! Point to each number as you count from 1 to 10.

FS-32055 Kindergarten Review

What a Pair!

Connect the dots from **1** to **10**.

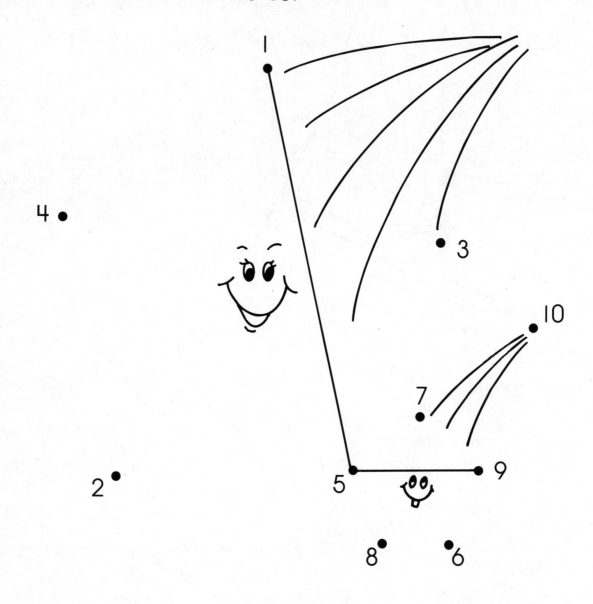

Try This! Point to each number as you count backwards from 10 to 1.

FS-32055 Kindergarten Review

Name

Number Boxes

Trace.

1	2	3	4	5
6	7	8	9	10
11	12	13	14	15
16	17	18	19	20

Write.

1				

Try This! Draw 20 flowers. Color them using only 2 different colors.

FS-32055 Kindergarten Review

Name_____

Happy Numbers

Color.

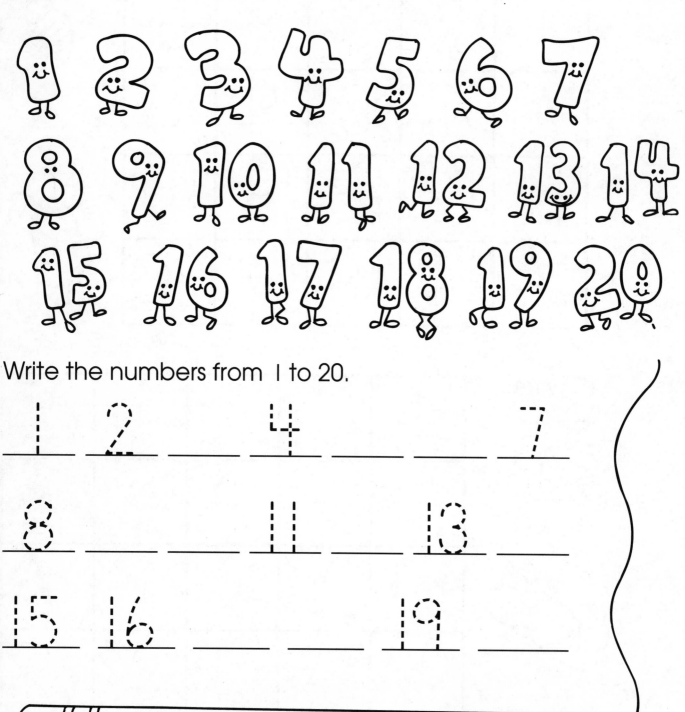

Write the numbers from 1 to 20.

Try This! Write the numbers from 11 to 20.

Name _____

A Long Time Ago

Connect the dots from **1** to **20**.

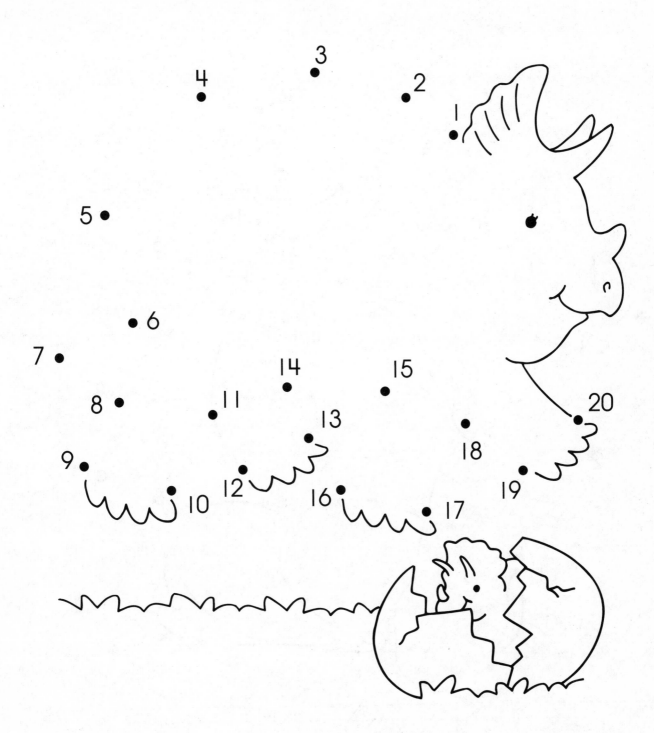

Try This! Point to each number as you count from 1 to 20.

FS-32055 Kindergarten Review

An Endangered Animal

Connect the dots from 1 to 20.

10
9
11
8
12
7
13
6
14
5
15
4
16
3
17
2
18
19
1
20

Try This! Point to each number as you count backwards from 20 to 1.

FS-32055 Kindergarten Review

Number Patterns

Find the number pattern.
Write the missing numbers.

1, 2, ___, 4, ___, 6, 7, ___, 9, 10

8, ___, 10, 11, ___, 13, 14, ___

10, 11, ___, 13, ___, 15, ___, 17

14, ___, 16, ___, 18, ___, 20

3, ___, 5, 6, 7, ___, 9, ___, ___

2, ___, 4, ___, 6, ___, 8, ___, 10

Try This! Pick 3 rows. Write the numbers that should come next.

FS-32055 Kindergarten Review

Missing Numbers
Find the number pattern.
Write the missing numbers.

0, 1, 2, ____, 4, ____, 6, ____, 8, 9

8, 9, ____, 11, 12, ____, 14, ____

12, 13, ____, ____, 16, 17, ____, 19

13, 14, ____, 16, ____, 18, ____, 20

____, 1, 2, ____, 4, ____, 6, 7, ____

1, ____, 3, ____, 5, ____, 7, ____, 9

Try This! Write a number pattern that goes backwards.

 FS-32055 Kindergarten Review

Add Them Up

Count. Write. Add.

2 + 3 = ___

___ + ___ = ___

___ + ___ = ___

___ + ___ = ___

  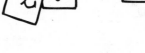

___ + ___ = ___

___ + ___ = ___

___ + ___ = ___

  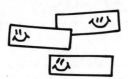

___ + ___ = ___

Try This! Draw a picture to match: 2 stars + 1 star = 3 stars

 FS-32055 Kindergarten Review

Sports Fun

Add. Write the math sentence.

1 + 3 = 4

___ + ___ = ___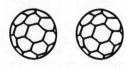

___ + ___ = ___

___ + ___ = ___

___ + ___ = ___

___ + ___ = ___

___ + ___ = ___

Try This! Write a problem whose answer is 5. ___ + ___ = 5

   FS-32055 Kindergarten Review

Buttons

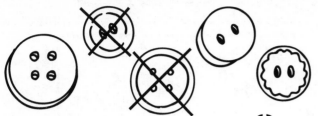

Cross out 2.
How many are left? **3**

Cross out 1.
How many are left?

Cross out 3.
How many are left?

Cross out 0.
How many are left?

Cross out 4.
How many are left?

Cross out 2.
How many are left?

Cross out 3.
How many are left?

Cross out 5.
How many are left?

Try This! Draw a picture to solve this problem: *You crossed out 2 buttons. 1 was left. How many buttons did you start with?*

FS-32055 Kindergarten Review

Dinosaurs

Cross out 4. How many are left?

Cross out 3. How many are left?

Cross out 0. How many are left?

Cross out 2. How many are left?

Cross out 1. How many are left?

Try This! You have 4 toy dinosaurs. You give a friend 2 of them.
Draw a picture that shows how many you each have now.

A Special Place

Draw a picture of a place you have visited. Trace and finish the sentence.

I went to

Try This! Tell someone about the place you visited.

Name _____

What a Day!

What did you like doing at school today?
Draw a picture of it. Finish the sentence.

At school today I liked

_____
- -
_____

_____
- -
_____

Try This! Find a class friend who wrote something different.

94

FS-32055 Kindergarten Review

What a Place!

Think of a real or make-believe place.
Draw a picture of it.
Write a sentence about it.

Try This! Let a friend guess if your place is real or pretend.

Name _____

A Very Important Person

Draw a picture of someone important to you.

Write a sentence about him or her.

Try This! Share your picture and sentence with a friend.

FS-32055 Kindergarten Review

The Day the Monster Came

A silly monster has come to school.
Draw a picture of it.
Write a question you would like to ask it.

?

Try This! Meet with a friend. Make up answers to each other's monster questions.

97

School Helpers

Draw a picture of someone who works at school.
Write a question you would like to ask him or her.

Try This! Find the person you drew. Ask your question.

    FS-32055 Kindergarten Review

Plan a Story—Characters

Draw a picture of the people or animals you will have in your story. Write their names.

Try This! Draw a star by the character who will do the most.

FS-32055 Kindergarten Review

Name_____

Plan a Story—Ideas

What will happen in the beginning of your story?
Draw a picture.

What will happen at the end of your story?
Draw a picture.

Try This! What will happen in the middle? Tell a friend.

100

Thank You!

Think of someone who helped you.
Make a card for him or her.

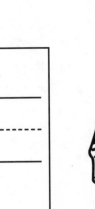

To
_____
- -
_____

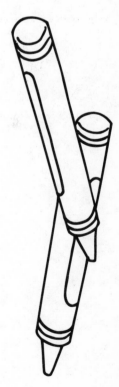

Thank you!

Try This! Plan a way to give the person your card.

FS-32055 Kindergarten Review

A Thank-you Note

Draw a picture showing how someone helped you.
Write **Thank you!** below it.

Try This! Think of a way you could help someone.

102

I Can Spell!
Make a list of words you
know how to spell.

Try This! Think of a word you want to learn to spell.
Try spelling it. Then find someone to help teach it to you.

Learning to Spell

Have someone help
you make a list of
words you want to
learn to spell.

Read
the word.
Spell it aloud.
Trace it.
Write it.

Try This! Say a word. Then close your eyes and spell it aloud.
Open your eyes and check your spelling.

My Favorite Part

Listen to a story. What story did you listen to?

Draw your favorite part.

Try This! Meet with a partner. Talk about your pictures.

The Best Part

Listen to a storybook. Draw your favorite part of the book.

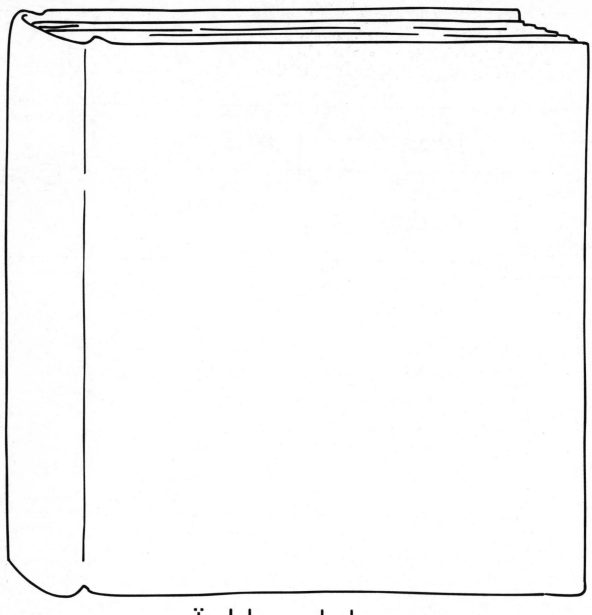

The part I liked best was

_____

- -

_____

Try This! Find someone who liked a different part of the book.

Name _____

That Doesn't Belong!

Color the pictures that belong in the group.
Draw an **X** on the picture that doesn't belong.

Try This! Think of another picture for each group.

FS-32055 Kindergarten Review

Sorry, Wrong Group

Color the pictures that belong in the group.
Draw an **X** on the picture that doesn't belong.

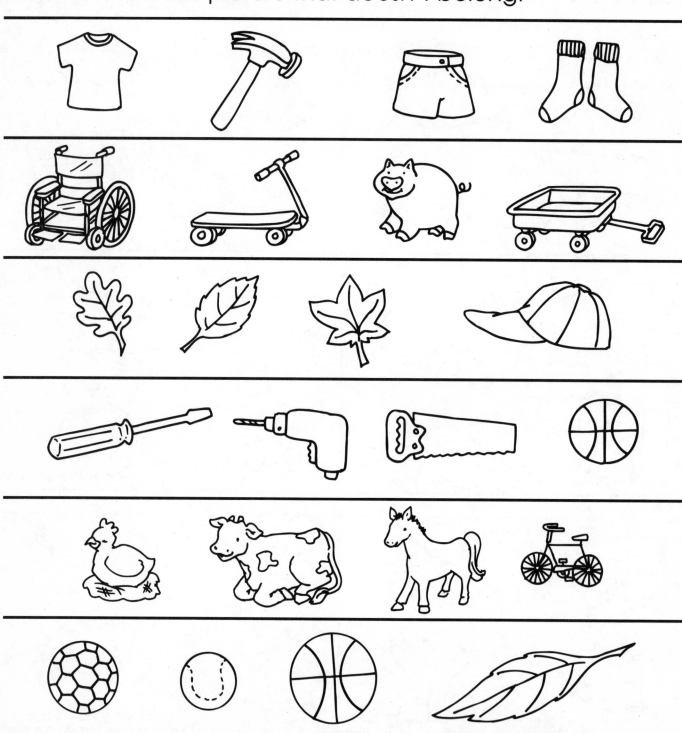

Try This! Choose a group. Draw another picture for it.

108

Name _____

Different and the Same

Do this page with a partner.
Look at each set of pictures.
Think of two ways they are different.
Then think of two ways they are the same.

For this set,
draw
yourself
and your
partner.

Try This! Think of someone else that is like you and your partner.

FS-32055 Kindergarten Review

How Are They the Same?

Look at the two pictures. How are they the same?
Tell or write an answer.

Both _____

Both _____

Both _____

Try This! Think of three ways the pictures are different.

FS-32055 Kindergarten Review

How to Draw a Turtle

Oops! The boxes are out of order.
Label the steps from **1** to **6**.

Try This! Follow the steps to draw a turtle.

FS-32055 Kindergarten Review

How to Draw a Whale

Oh, no! The boxes are out of order.
Label the steps from **1** to **6**.

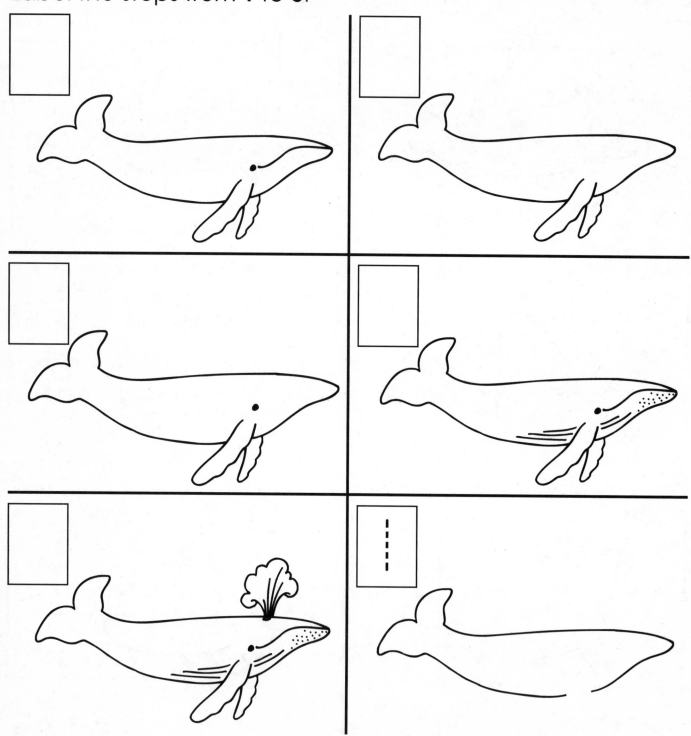

Try This! Follow the steps to draw a whale.

112

What Happens Next?

Look at the picture. Draw a line to the box that shows what happens next.

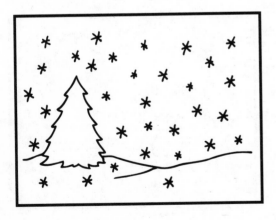

Try This! Draw a picture of you doing something kind. Then draw another picture that shows what might happen next.

Dinosaur Friends

Look at the picture. Draw a line to the box that shows what happens next.

Try This! Draw a picture of two sad dinosaurs. Then draw a picture that shows what happened that made them sad.

FS-32055 Kindergarten Review

Does It Belong?

Circle the five things in the picture that do not belong.
Color the picture.

$$+\frac{1}{2}$$

Try This! Draw a picture that shows a new child at school who is shy. Then act out what you would do to help the child.

FS-32055 Kindergarten Review

Solving a Problem

Look at the picture.
What do you think the problem is?
Draw a picture that shows one way to solve it.

Try This! Compare pictures with a partner.

Kindergarten

What do you like best about kindergarten?
Draw a picture. Finish the sentence.

The best part of kindergarten is

_____

- -

_____

- -

_____

Try This! How will first grade be different? Draw a picture.

FS-32055 Kindergarten Review

Name _____

My Teacher

Have you listened to the book *Miss Nelson Is Missing!*?
In that story, Miss Nelson is a nice teacher and
Miss Viola Swamp is a very mean teacher.
What is your teacher like?
Draw a picture of your teacher.
Think of two words that describe him or her.

Try This! What do you like best about your teacher? What do you think your teacher likes best about you?

FS-32055 Kindergarten Review

Super Star!

Draw yourself inside the star
doing something you like to do.
Write your name.

My name is

_____
- - - - - - - - - - - - - - - - - - - -
_____

_____
- - - - - - - - - - - - - - - - - - - -
_____

Try This! Meet with a friend. Read your papers together.

Someone Special

Finish the sentences.
Draw what you would like to do for your birthday.

My name is

_____

- -

_____

My birthday is

_____

- -

_____

Try This! Can you find someone whose birthday is in the same month as yours?

FS-32055 Kindergarten Review

Meet My Family

Finish the sentence. Draw a picture of your family.

There are _____ people in my family.
Here we are!

Try This! Write the name of someone in your family.

My Family

Finish the sentence. Draw a picture of your family.

My family is important to me because

_____

_____

_____

_____

Try This! Find a classmate who wrote something different.

Where I Live

Draw your home. Write your address.

My address is

_____

- -

_____

_____

- -

_____

Try This! Can you name two of your neighbors?

Home Safety

My name is
_____
- -
_____
- -
_____

My address is
_____
- -
_____
- -
_____

_____
- - - - - - -
If I need help, I can call _____

Try This! Meet with a friend. Pretend you called 911 or 0 for help. Practice saying your name and address in a clear voice.

My Phone Number

Write your phone number. Color the telephone.

My phone number is

_____

- -

_____

Try This! Meet with a friend. Practice telling your phone numbers to each other.

FS-32055 Kindergarten Review

Telephone Talk

Write your phone number.
Draw yourself talking politely on the telephone.

My phone number is

_____

- -

_____

Try This! Meet with a friend. Practice using good phone manners.

Meet My Friend

Draw a picture of yourself with a friend.
Finish the sentences.

I like my friend because

_____

- -

_____

My friend likes me because

_____

- -

_____

Try This! Meet with a partner.
Talk about what makes a good friend.

Super Kid Award

Color Super Kid to look like you. Finish the sentence.

I am a Super Kid because I

_____

- -

_____

Try This! Read the papers of other Super Kids in your class.